THE RICHARD RODGERS COLLECTION

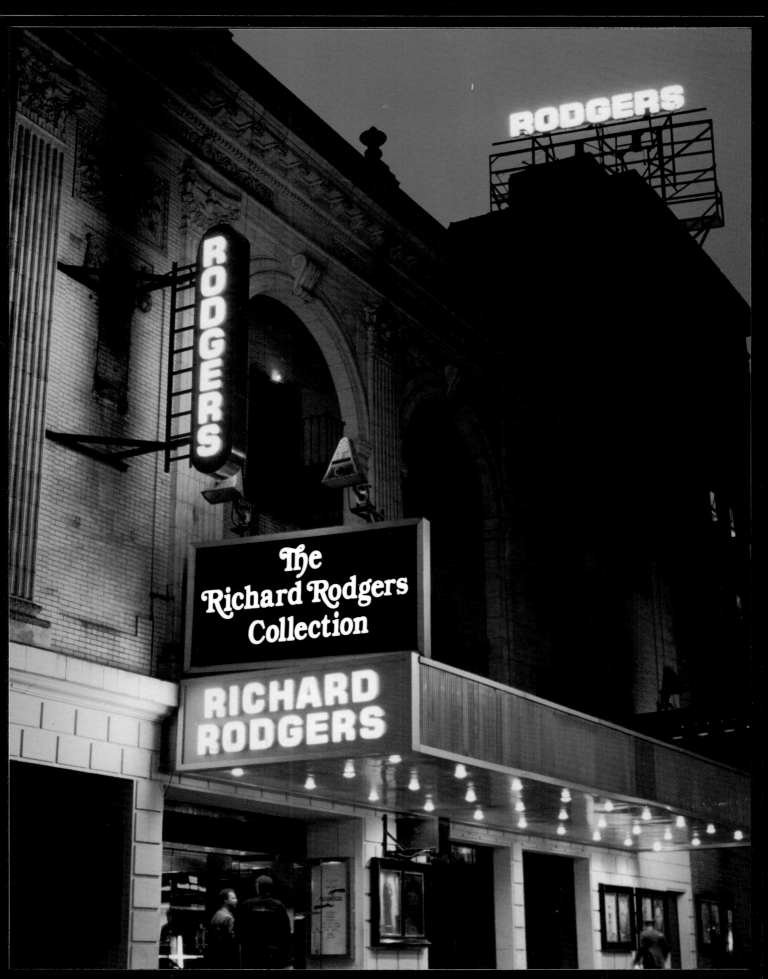

The Richard Rodgers Collection

RICHARD RODGERS

PIANO • VOCAL • GUITAR

THE RICHARD RODGERS COLLECTION

Richard Rodgers, 1959

A Joint Publication of

A RODGERS AND HAMMERSTEIN COMPANY

and

HAL•LEONARD
CORPORATION

7777 W. BLUEMOUND RD. P.O. BOX 13819 MILWAUKEE, WI 53213

*Cover designed by
Frank "Fraver" Verlizzo.*

Photo by Gary Denys.

Rodgers, Richard, 1902 – 1979
    [Musicals. Vocal scores. Selections]
    The Richard Rodgers collection.
    1 score.
    Songs from musicals.
    Acc. arr. for piano.
    Lyrics principally by Lorenz Hart or Oscar
    Hammerstein II.
    ISBN 0-7935-0033-8
    1. Musicals — Excerpts — Vocal scores with
    piano. I. Hart, Lorenz, 1895 - 1943.
    II. Hammerstein II, Oscar, 1895 – 1960.
    III. Title.
    M1507.R7R5   1990

WILLIAMSON MUSIC®

A RODGERS AND HAMMERSTEIN COMPANY

229 W. 28th St., 11th floor
New York, New York 10001
Telephone: (212)564-4000
Facsimile: (212)268-1245

CONTENTS

Richard and Dorothy Rodgers (1972)

PREFACE

by Dorothy Rodgers

When I was asked to suggest some of my favorites among Dick's songs for inclusion in this Collection, I found myself remembering his answer when interviewers or fans asked him the same question. He would explain that it was a little like being asked to name your favorite child. Then, if pressed, he would say with a deprecating smile: "The last one I wrote!"

I am overwhelmed when I think about the outpouring of melody that flowed from his limitless creativity, but I did manage to choose at least a good many of my favorites for this volume, including some lesser-known songs. Now, ten years after Dick's death, his works continue to be played around the world, in theatres and concert halls, in films, on television and on cassettes both audio and visual.

On March 27th, 1990, Broadway's 46th Street Theatre was re-named for him, a tribute from the theatre's owner, James Nederlander, following a suggestion made by an old friend of Dick's and mine, Alexander Cohen.

Recently a friend asked me when Dick first knew he had "made it." No one had ever asked me that before so I had no ready answer. I thought about it for a while and then realized that in the arts there never is any such single moment for anyone to know the answer. Given the built-in insecurity in the theatre world and of those who labor in its vineyard, my answer to the question must be that there was no *one* moment when Dick thought he "had it made." He had many such moments.

He loved the theatre and he loved writing music for it. It was wonderful that during his lifetime he was able to enjoy knowing the great pleasure he had given to so many. And he never forgot how great it was to smell the flowers.

Dorothy Rodgers

September, 1990

REMEMBERING THE MAESTRO OF BROADWAY

by Stephen Holden

This article first appeared in *The New York Times* on Sunday, April 22, 1990.
Copyright © 1990 by The New York Times Company
Reprinted by Permission

"People used to say to Dick, especially after *Oklahoma!* 'You'll never write anything as good as that again,'" Dorothy Rodgers recalled recently. "I know they meant to be kind, but it hit home, and he used to worry about whether he was going to be able to write. When he had gotten the first number done on a new show, he had an expression. He used to say the first olive was out of the jar."

The widow of the composer Richard Rodgers was reminiscing about her husband, who died on Dec. 30, 1979, at 77 following his third bout with cancer. His death came just two months short of their 50th wedding anniversary. Sitting in the library of her midtown Manhattan hotel suite, surrounded by memorabilia, including framed photographs of the couple's six grown grandchildren, Mrs. Rodgers displayed an acute memory for times past and an extensive knowledge of musical theater history. For nearly 50 years she was at the side of the man who, perhaps more than any other composer, oversaw the American musical theater's coming of age.

Between 1920 and 1959, first with Lorenz Hart and then with Oscar Hammerstein II, Rodgers composed the music for more than 40 Broadway shows, including *On Your Toes, Babes In Arms, Pal Joey* (with Hart, who died in 1943), *Oklahoma!, Carousel, South Pacific, The King and I* and *The Sound of Music* (with Hammerstein, who died in 1960). After Hammerstein's death Rodgers continued to create for Broadway, writing his own lyrics for *No Strings,* and in the final years collaborating with Stephen Sondheim, Sheldon Harnick and Martin Charnin.

The list of Richard Rodgers songs considered standards is rivaled only by that of Irving Berlin and George Gershwin and includes "My Funny Valentine," "Where or When" and "Bewitched" (with Hart) and "If I Loved You," "You'll Never Walk Alone" and "Some Enchanted Evening" (with Hammerstein). The songs with Hart tended to be intimate, wry and bittersweet as compared with the grander, more formal ballads he wrote with Hammerstein.

Of his shows, Mrs. Rodgers said her husband "was proudest of *Carousel,* because he felt it cut deeper and moved people more, and he liked the way some of the songs were not held down to 32 bars so that whole scenes were like musical plays."

Although Rodgers' music and the form of his shows became more operatic as the years passed, the composer didn't like opera itself, "which was lucky for me," Mrs. Rodgers said, "because I was bored to death by it. But he loved the symphony. Brahms was his favorite."

Rodgers was a major innovator: the 1936 show *On Your Toes,* with its George Balanchine choreography, brought ballet to the Broadway musical stage, while the seamless blend of music, lyrics, libretto and choreography in *Oklahoma!* defined what was called "lyric theater." Yet, Mrs. Rodgers said, he entertained no grand schemes to revolutionize his field.

"I don't think Dick and Larry or Dick and Oscar thought in terms of breaking through or doing a new kind of theater," she said. "They just wanted to do something that hadn't been done and that was fresh. Dick always felt that the way people used to copy their hit shows of the previous season was the worst thing you could do and was a guarantee of failure."

As prolific as he was, Mrs. Rodgers said, her husband never wrote songs independent of dramatic context. And none of them, she added, were directly inspired by personal experience.

"He was really a man who wrote for situations and characters and knew exactly what he wanted to convey to the audience through a particular song" she emphasized.

"He usually had some knowledge before he sat down to write, such as who was going to sing it, what the singer's range was and what the mood would be. If he wrote something that had a lovely melody but that didn't work in the show, he never had any qualms about taking it out. Neither did Oscar or Larry, and they seldom bothered to use them over."

As for the collaborative process itself, Lorenz Hart "was about the best read person I ever met," she recalled. "He was brilliant and we loved him, but he was difficult. Some times he would disappear while you were talking to him. When he and Dick worked he would never put pencil to paper until Dick had finished a tune. And Dick always had to stay in the room while Larry was working. Dick said that all the lyrics were written on the stationery of defunct companies with grand-sounding names that Larry's father had started.

"Oscar, on the other hand, was meticulous, methodical and dependable. He liked having the freedom to write his lyrics before Dick set them. And Dick didn't really care which way he worked. He adapted very easily. I used to think that, given equal talent for writing music and lyrics, it was harder to write the lyrics. Writing music seemed to be a kind of magic that happened in front of my eyes. But I could understand the difficulty of trying to find a new way of saying 'I love you.'"

Rodgers' bushy-browed aristocratic look, along with his stature as a composer, helped to foster a public image of him as a forbidding Olympic figure for whom composing music and doing business were synonymous.

That image, Mrs. Rodgers insisted, did not reflect the real person. "Dick had a wonderful sense of humor," she said. "This was something that most people who didn't know him couldn't understand because he could look very stern, and when he was concentrating he would knit his brows so you might think he was angry. But he wasn't. Dick was always portrayed as a man who looked like a banker and who was a businessman. But he was not a businessman. He loved every aspect of the theater except the business aspect, which he was happy to pay other people to take care of..."

...Of all the turning points in Rodgers' career, the most critical was the transition between major collaborators. Hart who was drinking heavily, had been offered the job of helping turn the play *Green Grow The Lilacs* into *Oklahoma!* but said he wasn't interested.

"Dick told him that if he didn't want to do it he was going to do it with somebody else, and said he had Oscar in mind," Mrs. Rodgers recalled. "Larry said fine. But even before Larry turned it down, Oscar had been so eager to do it that he had volunteered to finish it, if necessary, without taking the credit.

"Everybody connected with *Oklahoma!* except Dick had been unsuccessful for many years," she went on. "The Theater Guild, which produced the show, was almost out of business. The original play, *Green Grows the Lilacs* had not been a success, and Oscar hadn't had a success for about 10 years. Agnes de Mille had never done a theater piece, and when the ticket brokers who went up to New Haven to see it came back, they predicted bad reviews.

"Just before they left town, they had a run-through in New York, and I went to it. There was just one light on a bare stage and no sets and no costumes. Afterward, Dick and Oscar and Agnes and Rouben Mamoulian got together to discuss what they thought. Dick put me in a cab. I went home and wrote a note, which I put on his pillow. It said this is the best thing I've ever seen in my life."

RICHARD RODGERS

A Biographical Sketch

Richard Rodgers' contribution to the musical theatre of his day was extraordinary, and his influence on the musical theatre of today and tomorrow is legendary. His career spanned more than six decades, and his hits ranged from the silver screens of Hollywood to the bright lights of Broadway, London and beyond. He was the recipient of countless awards, including Pulitzers, Tonys, Oscars, Emmys and Grammys. He wrote more than 900 published songs, and forty Broadway musicals.

Richard Rodgers was born in New York City on June 28, 1902. From 1920 to 1943 his professional credits included a series of musicals on Broadway, in London and in Hollywood written exclusively with lyricist Lorenz Hart. Starting with *Poor Little Ritz Girl* in 1920, their output throughout the decade featured an average of two new shows a season. After spending the years 1931 to 1935 in Hollywood (where they wrote the scores for several feature films including the classic *Love Me Tonight* starring Maurice Chevalier) they returned to New York to compose the score for Billy Rose's circus extravaganza, *Jumbo*.

A golden period followed — golden for Rodgers & Hart, and golden for the American musical: *On Your Toes* (1936), *Babes In Arms* (1937), *I'd Rather Right* (1937), *I Married an Angel* (1938), *The Boys From Syracuse* (1938), *Too Many Girls* (1939), *Higher and Higher* (1940), *Pal Joey* (1940) and *By Jupiter* (1942).

The chemistry of the Rodgers & Hart collaboration resulted in a potent blend of wit and pathos, with melodies that were sophisticated, humorous and romantic. The partnership ended with the death of Lorenz Hart in 1943, but the legacy of songs remains: "Manhattan," "Mountain Greenery," "My Heart Stood Still," "Isn't It Romantic?" "Blue Moon," "There's a Small Hotel," "I Wish I Were In Love Again," "My Funny Valentine," "Where Or When," "Falling In Love With Love," "This Can't Be Love," "I Didn't Know What Time It Was," "It Never Entered My Mind," "Bewitched" and "I Could Write a Book."

In 1943 Richard Rodgers joined forces with lyricist and author Oscar Hammerstein II, whose work in the field of operetta throughout the '20s and '30s had been as groundbreaking as had Rodgers' work in the field of musical comedy (with such successes as *Rose-Marie*, *The Desert Song*, *The New Moon* and the milestone *Show Boat* to his credit). The Rodgers & Hammerstein partnership resulted in an entirely new genre, the musical play, and their first entry out of the starting gate was the landmark *Oklahoma!*

Oklahoma! launched an extraordinary era in the American musical theatre, to which Rodgers & Hammerstein contributed the following musical plays: *Carousel* (1945), *Allegro* (1947), *South Pacific* (1949), *The King and I* (1951), *Me and Juliet* (1953), *Pipe Dream* (1955), *Flower Drum Song* (1958) and *The Sound of Music* (1959). They also wrote the score for the 1945 movie musical *State Fair* and the 1957 television musical *Cinderella*.

These musicals harvested a rich bounty of songs that are renowned not only as Broadway showstoppers but as classics of American popular song as well, including: "Oh, What a Beautiful Mornin'," "People Will Say We're In Love," "The Surrey With The Fringe on Top," "Oklahoma," "If I Loved

You," "You'll Never Walk Alone," "It Might As Well Be Spring," "It's A Grand Night For Singing," "Bali Ha'i," "Some Enchanted Evening," "There Is Nothin' Like a Dame," "Getting To Know You," "I Have Dreamed," "Shall We Dance?" "No Other Love," "The Sound of Music," "Climb Ev'ry Mountain," "My Favorite Things" and "Edelweiss."

Richard Rodgers did venture beyond the musical theatre during his two primary collaborations, highlighted by the 1939 ballet *Ghost Town*, and the score for the 1952 NBC documentary series, *Victory At Sea*, the latter earning him an Emmy, a Gold Record and a Commendation from the U.S. Navy.

Following the death of Oscar Hammerstein II in the summer of 1960, Rodgers made a few more excursions beyond the field of stage musicals: in 1960 he composed the score for a second television documentary, *The Valiant Years*, about the life of Winston Churchill, and in 1967 he wrote music and lyrics for an NBC-TV adaptation of Bernard Shaw's *Androcles and the Lion.*

But he continued to write for the Broadway stage first and foremost, starting with *No Strings* in 1962 (for which he wrote both music and lyrics) and followed by *Do I Hear a Waltz?* (lyrics by Stephen Sondheim, 1965), *Two By Two* (lyrics by Martin Charnin, 1970), *Rex* (lyrics by Sheldon Harnick, 1976) and *I Remember Mama* (lyrics by Martin Charnin and Raymond Jessel, 1979).

Less than eight months after *I Remember Mama* opened on Broadway, Richard Rodgers died in his home in New York City on December 30, 1979. He was 77 years old.

On March 27, 1990, Richard Rodgers was honored posthumously with Broadway's highest accolade when the 46th Street Theatre, owned and operated by the Nederlander Organization, was renamed The Richard Rodgers Theatre. The theatre is home to The Richard Rodgers Gallery, a permanent exhibit in the lobby areas presented by ASCAP which honors the composer's life and works.

— Bert Fink
Director of Special Projects
Rodgers & Hammerstein

RICHARD RODGERS

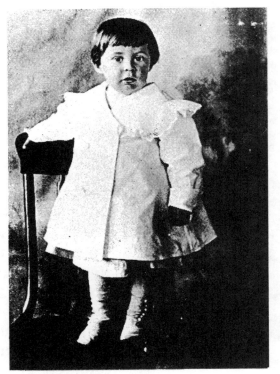

Age One

Family Portrait, 1905

Late teens

Mid 1920's

Richard Rodgers and Lorenz Hart

MANHATTAN
from The Broadway Musical GARRICK GAIETIES

Words by LORENZ HART
Music by RICHARD RODGERS

14

MOUNTAIN GREENERY

from The Broadway Musical THE GARRICK GAIETIES

Words by LORENZ HART
Music by RICHARD RODGERS

Richard Rodgers, Lorenz Hart and John, their
canine escort, on the BERENGARIA, 1927

MY HEART STOOD STILL
from ONE DAM THING AFTER ANOTHER

Words by LORENZ HART
Music by RICHARD RODGERS

YOU TOOK ADVANTAGE OF ME

from PRESENT ARMS

Words by LORENZ HART
Music by RICHARD RODGERS

WITH A SONG IN MY HEART

from SPRING IS HERE

Words by LORENZ HART
Music by RICHARD RODGERS

HE WAS TOO GOOD TO ME

from SIMPLE SIMON

Words by LORENZ HART
Music by RICHARD RODGERS

TEN CENTS A DANCE
from SIMPLE SIMON

Words by LORENZ HART
Music by RICHARD RODGERS

I work at the Pal-ace Ball-room, But, gee, that pal-ace is cheap; When I get back to my chil-ly hall room I'm much too tir-ed to sleep, I'm one of those la-dy teach-ers, A beau-ti-ful host-ess, you know, One

ISN'T IT ROMANTIC?

from The Paramount Picture LOVE ME TONIGHT

Words by LORENZ HART
Music by RICHARD RODGERS

I've nev-er met you, Yet nev-er
My face is glow-ing, I'm en-er-

doubt, dear, I can't for-get you, I've thought you out dear, I know your
get-ic, The art of sew-ing, I found po-et-ic, My nee-dle

pro-file and I know the way you kiss just the thing I
punc-tu-ates the rhy-thm of ro-mance! I don't give a

46

LOVER
from The Paramount Picture LOVE ME TONIGHT

Words by LORENZ HART
Music by RICHARD RODGERS

BLUE MOON

Words by LORENZ HART
Music by RICHARD RODGERS

IT'S EASY TO REMEMBER

from The Paramount Picture MISSISSIPPI

Words by LORENZ HART
Music by RICHARD RODGERS

With you___ I owned the earth. With you___ I ruled cre - a - tion. No

you,___ and what's it worth? It's just an im - i - ta - tion.___

Slowly and expressively

Guitar Tacet

Your sweet ex - pres - sion,___ the smile you gave me,___ the way you looked when we

THE MOST BEAUTIFUL GIRL IN THE WORLD

from JUMBO

Words by LORENZ HART
Music by RICHARD RODGERS

63

LITTLE GIRL BLUE

from JUMBO

Words by LORENZ HART
Music by RICHARD RODGERS

OVER AND OVER AGAIN

from JUMBO

Words by LORENZ HART
Music by RICHARD RODGERS

gain. A star does not come out of the sky, He starts to

work at ten._____ To reach the top you've got to keep

try - ing o - ver and o - ver a - gain._____

TRIO

Up in the morn-ing and down in the ring a - cro-bat, rid - er and

68

THERE'S A SMALL HOTEL
from ON YOUR TOES

Words by LORENZ HART
Music by RICHARD RODGERS

He: A cer-tain place I know, Frank-ie, Where fun-ny peo-ple can have fun.

That's where we two will go, Dar-ling, Be-fore you can count up One, Two, Three. For:

REFRAIN

There's a small ho-tel With a wish-ing well; I

wish that we were there to-geth - er. _____

I WISH I WERE IN LOVE AGAIN
from BABES IN ARMS

Words by LORENZ HART
Music by RICHARD RODGERS

You don't know that I felt good When we up and part-ed.

You don't know I knocked on wood, Glad-ly brok-en heart-ed.

Wor-ry-ing is through, I sleep all night,— Ap-pe-tite and health re-stored.

You don't know how much I'm bored!

REFRAIN

1. The sleep-less nights, The dai-ly fights, The quick to-bog-gan when you
2. (The) fur-tive sigh, The black-ened eye, The words "I'll love you till the

reach the heights; I miss the kiss-es and I miss the bites, I
day I die," The self-de-cep-tion that be-lieves the lie, I

THE LADY IS A TRAMP
from BABES IN ARMS

Words by LORENZ HART
Music by RICHARD RODGERS

80

MY FUNNY VALENTINE

from BABES IN ARMS

Words by LORENZ HART
Music by RICHARD RODGERS

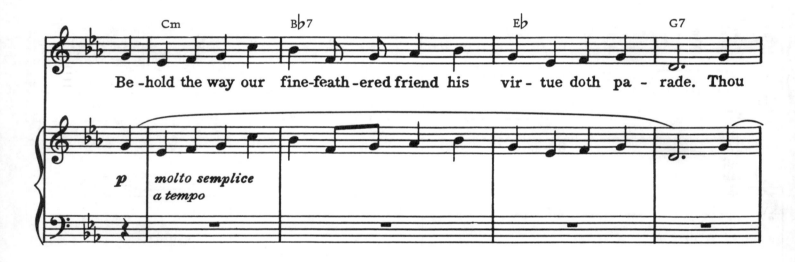

Be-hold the way our fine-feath-ered friend his vir-tue doth pa-rade. Thou

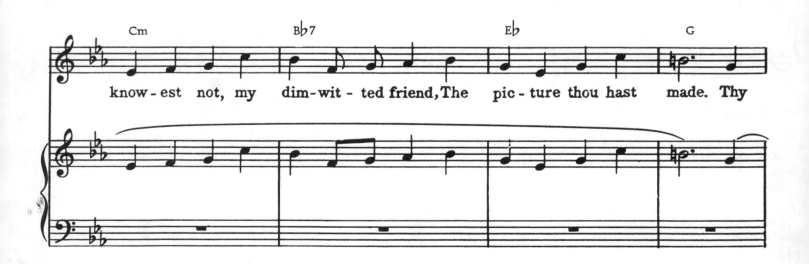

know-est not, my dim-wit-ted friend, The pic-ture thou hast made. Thy

WHERE OR WHEN

from BABES IN ARMS

Words by LORENZ HART
Music by RICHARD RODGERS

FALLING IN LOVE WITH LOVE

from THE BOYS FROM SYRACUSE

Words by LORENZ HART
Music by RICHARD RODGERS

SPRING IS HERE
from I MARRIED AN ANGEL

Words by LORENZ HART
Music by RICHARD RODGERS

THIS CAN'T BE LOVE

from THE BOYS FROM SYRACUSE

Words by LORENZ HART
Music by RICHARD RODGERS

beat! This is too sweet to be love. This can't be love be-cause I feel so well;—— But still I love to look—— in your eyes.—— eyes.

I DIDN'T KNOW WHAT TIME IT WAS

from TOO MANY GIRLS

Words by LORENZ HART
Music by RICHARD RODGERS

I COULD WRITE A BOOK

from PAL JOEY

Words by LORENZ HART
Music by RICHARD RODGERS

IT NEVER ENTERED MY MIND
from HIGHER AND HIGHER

Lyrics by LORENZ HART
Music by RICHARD RODGERS

walk in a daze now, I nev-er go to shows at night, But just to ma-tin-ees now.

I see the show and home I go.

REFRAIN

Once I laughed when I heard you say-ing That I'd be play-ing

sol - i -taire,_ Un-eas-y in my eas-y chair._

YOU'RE NEARER

from TOO MANY GIRLS

Words by LORENZ HART
Music by RICHARD RODGERS

BEWITCHED
from PAL JOEY

Words by LORENZ HART
Music by RICHARD RODGERS

He's a fool and don't I know it, But a fool can have his charms;

I'm in love and don't I show it, Like a babe in arms.

WAIT TILL YOU SEE HER

from BY JUPITER

Words by LORENZ HART
Music by RICHARD RODGERS

OH, WHAT A BEAUTIFUL MORNIN'

from OKLAHOMA!

Lyrics by OSCAR HAMMERSTEIN II
Music by RICHARD RODGERS

1. There's a bright gold - en haze on the mead - ow
2. (All the) cat - tle are stand - in' like stat - ues
3. (All the) sounds of the earth are like mu - sic

There's a bright gold - en haze on the
All the bright cat - tle are stand - in' like
All the sounds of the earth are like

THE SURREY WITH THE FRINGE ON TOP

from OKLAHOMA!

Lyrics by OSCAR HAMMERSTEIN II
Music by RICHARD RODGERS

When I take you out, to-night, with me, _____

Hon-ey, here's the way it's goin' to be: _____

You will set be-hind a team of snow-white hors - es,

In the slick - est gig you ev - er see! ___

REFRAIN

Chicks and ducks and geese bet - ter scur - ry, When I take you
All the world - 'll fly in a flur - ry, When I take you
I can see the stars get - tin' blur - ry, When we drive back

out in the sur - rey, When I take you out in the sur - rey with the
out in the sur - rey, When I take you out in the sur - rey with the
home in the sur - rey, Driv - in' slow - ly home in the sur - rey with the

PEOPLE WILL SAY WE'RE IN LOVE

from OKLAHOMA!

Lyrics by OSCAR HAMMERSTEIN II
Music by RICHARD RODGERS

1. Why do they think up stor-ies that link my name with yours?
2. Some peo-ple claim that you are to blame as much as I

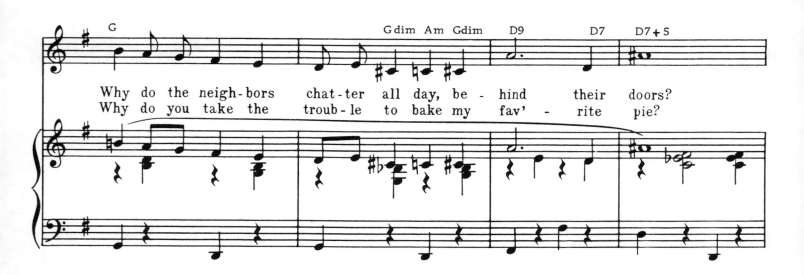

Why do the neigh-bors chat-ter all day, be-hind their doors?
Why do you take the troub-le to bake my fav'-rite pie?

OKLAHOMA
from OKLAHOMA!

Lyrics by OSCAR HAMMERSTEIN II
Music by RICHARD RODGERS

* Names of chords for Ukulele and Banjo.
Symbols for Guitar.

IF I LOVED YOU
from CAROUSEL

Lyrics by OSCAR HAMMERSTEIN II
Music by RICHARD RODGERS

When I worked in the mill, Weav-in' at the loom, I'd gaze ab-sent-
Kind-a scraw-ny and pale, Pick-in' at my food And love-sick like

mind-ed at the roof _____ And half the time the shut-tle 'd
an-y oth-er guy _____ I'd throw a-way my sweat-er and

tan-gle in the threads, And the warp 'd get mixed with the woof _____
dress up like a dude In a dick-ey and a col-lar and a tie _____

WHAT'S THE USE OF WOND'RIN'

from CAROUSEL

Lyrics by OSCAR HAMMERSTEIN II
Music by RICHARD RODGERS

What's the use of won-'drin' if he's good or if he's bad, Or if you like the way he wears his hat? Oh! what's the use of won-'drin', If he's good or If he's bad? He's your fel-ler and you love him.__ That's all there is to that.__

YOU'LL NEVER WALK ALONE
from CAROUSEL

Lyrics by OSCAR HAMMERSTEIN II
Music by RICHARD RODGERS

IT MIGHT AS WELL BE SPRING

from STATE FAIR

Lyrics by OSCAR HAMMERSTEIN II
Music by RICHARD RODGERS

IT'S A GRAND NIGHT FOR SINGING

from STATE FAIR

Lyrics by OSCAR HAMMERSTEIN II
Music by RICHARD RODGERS

Richard Rodgers at a rehearsal of ALLEGRO with
Agnes de Mille, far right, in 1947.

(from l. to r.) Joshua Logan, Richard Rodgers, Oscar Hammerstein II, Mary Martin and James Michener in preparation for SOUTH PACIFIC (1949).

SOME ENCHANTED EVENING
from SOUTH PACIFIC

Lyrics by OSCAR HAMMERSTEIN II
Music by RICHARD RODGERS

THERE IS NOTHIN' LIKE A DAME

from SOUTH PACIFIC

Lyrics by OSCAR HAMMERSTEIN II
Music by RICHARD RODGERS

BALI HA'I
from SOUTH PACIFIC

Lyrics by OSCAR HAMMERSTEIN II
Music by RICHARD RODGERS

I'M GONNA WASH THAT MAN RIGHT OUTA MY HAIR

from SOUTH PACIFIC

Lyrics by OSCAR HAMMERSTEIN II
Music by RICHARD RODGERS

YOUNGER THAN SPRINGTIME

from SOUTH PACIFIC

Lyrics by OSCAR HAMMERSTEIN II
Music by RICHARD RODGERS

YOU'VE GOT TO BE CAREFULLY TAUGHT

from SOUTH PACIFIC

Lyrics by OSCAR HAMMERSTEIN II
Music by RICHARD RODGERS

Allegro con spirito

You've got to be taught to hate and fear. You've got to be taught from year to year. It's got to be drummed in your dear lit-tle ear. You've got to be care-ful-ly

THIS NEARLY WAS MINE

from SOUTH PACIFIC

Lyrics by OSCAR HAMMERSTEIN II
Music by RICHARD RODGERS

Richard Rodgers and Oscar Hammerstein II (1951).

*Richard Rodgers, Oscar Hammerstein II and
Gertrude Lawrence as "Anna" rehearsing a KING
AND I segment for television, 1951*

HELLO, YOUNG LOVERS
from THE KING AND I

Lyrics by OSCAR HAMMERSTEIN II
Music by RICHARD RODGERS

GETTING TO KNOW YOU
from THE KING AND I

Lyrics by OSCAR HAMMERSTEIN II
Music by RICHARD RODGERS

It's a ver-y an-cient say-ing But a true and hon-est thought, That if you be-come a teach-er, by your pu-pils you'll be taught. As a teach-er, I've been

I HAVE DREAMED
from THE KING AND I

Lyrics by OSCAR HAMMERSTEIN II
Music by RICHARD RODGERS

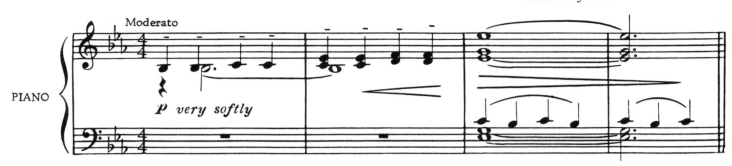

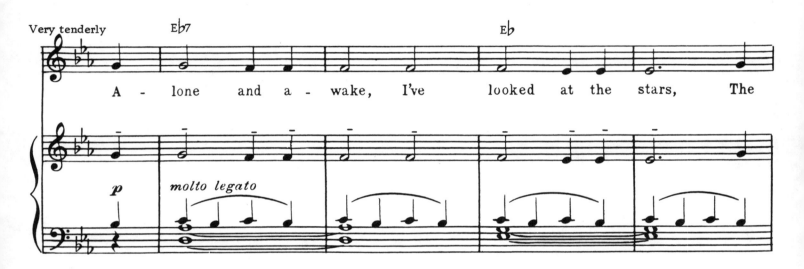

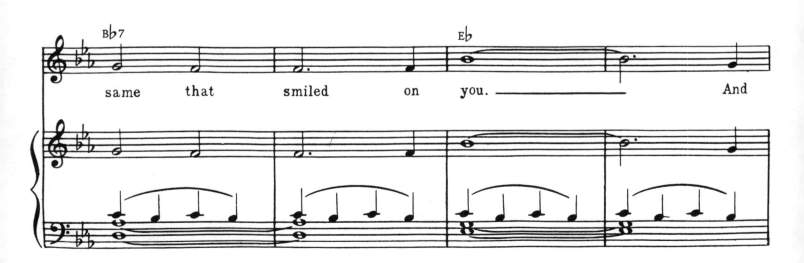

SHALL WE DANCE?
from THE KING AND I

Lyrics by OSCAR HAMMERSTEIN II
Music by RICHARD RODGERS

NO OTHER LOVE
from ME AND JULIET

Lyrics by OSCAR HAMMERSTEIN II
Music by RICHARD RODGERS

Richard Rodgers listening to a playback of the television soundtrack recording for "Victory at Sea" (1952)

Julie Andrews with Oscar Hammerstein II and
Richard Rodgers, during rehearsals for
"CINDERELLA", CBS-TV, March 31, 1957.

IN MY OWN LITTLE CORNER

from CINDERELLA

Lyrics by OSCAR HAMMERSTEIN II
Music by RICHARD RODGERS

TEN MINUTES AGO
from CINDERELLA

Lyrics by OSCAR HAMMERSTEIN II
Music by RICHARD RODGERS

*Richard Rodgers, Oscar Hammerstein II and Dorothy
Rodgers at the Broadway opening of FLOWER DRUM
SONG (1958).*

Pat Suzuki, Miyoshi Umeki and Richard Rodgers during rehearsal of FLOWER DRUM SONG, 1958.

LOVE, LOOK AWAY
from FLOWER DRUM SONG

Lyrics by OSCAR HAMMERSTEIN II
Music by RICHARD RODGERS

Mary Martin and Richard Rodgers listen to a
playback during the recording of the original
Broadway cast album for THE SOUND OF MUSIC
(1959).

THE SOUND OF MUSIC
from THE SOUND OF MUSIC

Lyrics by OSCAR HAMMERSTEIN II
Music by RICHARD RODGERS

one more love-ly thing that the hills might say.

REFRAIN (moderately, with warm expression)

The hills are a-live with the sound of mu - sic, __ With songs they have sung for a thou - sand years. ___ The hills fill my heart with the sound of

MY FAVORITE THINGS
from THE SOUND OF MUSIC

Lyrics by OSCAR HAMMERSTEIN II
Music by RICHARD RODGERS

When I'm feel - ing sad, _____ I sim - ply re - mem - ber my fa - vor - ite things and then I don't feel so bad. _____

Oscar Hammerstein II, Mary Martin and Richard Rodgers backstage during THE SOUND OF MUSIC (1959)

CLIMB EV'RY MOUNTAIN
from THE SOUND OF MUSIC

Lyrics by OSCAR HAMMERSTEIN II
Music by RICHARD RODGERS

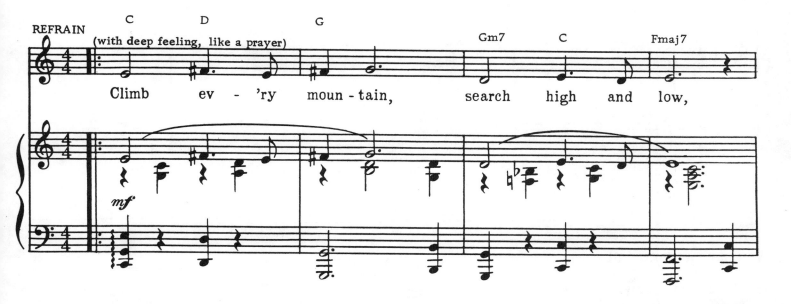

Climb ev - 'ry moun - tain, search high and low,

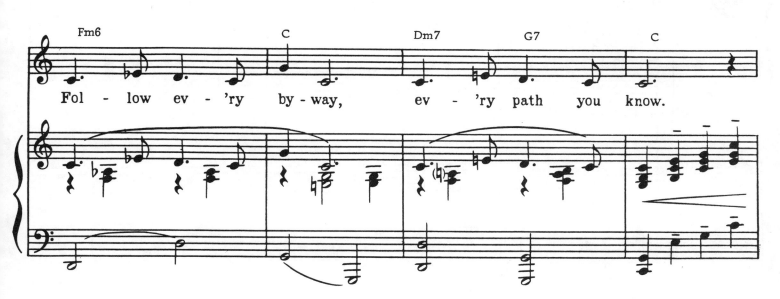

Fol - low ev - 'ry by - way, ev - 'ry path you know.

SIXTEEN GOING ON SEVENTEEN
from THE SOUND OF MUSIC

Lyrics by OSCAR HAMMERSTEIN II
Music by RICHARD RODGERS

Interlude

bell is no bell till you ring it, A song is no song till you sing it, And love in your heart was-n't put there to stay, Love is-n't love till you give it a-way.

3rd Refrain *(Assai moderato)*

When you're six-teen, go-ing on sev-en-teen,

Wait-ing for life to start, Some-bod-y kind who

touch-es your mind will sud-den-ly touch your heart!

When that hap-pens, af-ter it hap-pens, noth-ing is quite the

EDELWEISS
from THE SOUND OF MUSIC

Lyrics by OSCAR HAMMERSTEIN II
Music by RICHARD RODGERS

THE SWEETEST SOUNDS

from NO STRINGS

Lyrics and Music by
RICHARD RODGERS

Diahann Carroll, Richard Rodgers and Richard Kiley backstage after the opening night performance of NO STRINGS on Broadway (1962)

Composer Richard Rodgers (seated at piano), with (from l. to r.) author Arthur Laurents and lyricist Stephen Sondheim, working on DO I HEAR A WALTZ? (1965).

DO I HEAR A WALTZ?

from DO I HEAR A WALTZ?

Music by RICHARD RODGERS
Lyrics by STEPHEN SONDHEIM

Richard Rodgers with Sheldon Harnick preparing REX , 1976

AWAY FROM YOU

from REX

Lyrics by SHELDON HARNICK
Music by RICHARD RODGERS

Liv Ullman, Martin Charnin and Richard Rodgers
during rehearsals for I REMEMBER MAMA (1979).

Richard and Dorothy Rodgers at home in Fairfield, CT (1967)

Photo: Helen Marcus

YOU COULD NOT PLEASE ME MORE

from I REMEMBER MAMA *Words and Music by MARTIN CHARNIN and RICHARD RODGERS*

MCA music publishing

TIME
from I REMEMBER MAMA

Words and Music by MARTIN CHARNIN
and RICHARD RODGERS

When did it hap-pen? Where were we look-ing? What were we list-'ning to?_____ See how you shine now, hear how you speak now. Our hearts are so filled with you._____

MCA music publishing

The Richard Rodgers Collection

AWAY FROM YOU

BALI HA'I

BEWITCHED

BLUE MOON

CLIMB EV'RY MOUNTAIN

DO I HEAR A WALTZ?

EDELWEISS

FALLING IN LOVE WITH LOVE

GETTING TO KNOW YOU

HE WAS TOO GOOD TO ME

HELLO, YOUNG LOVERS

I COULD WRITE A BOOK

I DIDN'T KNOW
WHAT TIME IT WAS

I HAVE DREAMED

I WISH I WERE IN LOVE AGAIN

I'M GONNA WASH THAT MAN
RIGHT OUTA MY HAIR

IF I LOVED YOU

ISN'T IT ROMANTIC

IT MIGHT AS WELL BE SPRING

IT NEVER ENTERED MY MIND

IT'S A GRAND NIGHT
FOR SINGING

IT'S EASY TO REMEMBER

THE LADY IS A TRAMP

LITTLE GIRL BLUE

LOVE, LOOK AWAY

LOVER

MANHATTAN

THE MOST BEAUTIFUL GIRL
IN THE WORLD

MOUNTAIN GREENERY

MY FAVORITE THINGS

MY FUNNY VALENTINE

MY HEART STOOD STILL

NO OTHER LOVE

OH, WHAT A
BEAUTIFUL MORNIN'

OKLAHOMA

OVER AND OVER AGAIN

PEOPLE WILL SAY
WE'RE IN LOVE

SHALL WE DANCE?

SIXTEEN GOING ON
SEVENTEEN

SOME ENCHANTED EVENING

THE SOUND OF MUSIC

SPRING IS HERE

THE SURREY WITH THE
FRINGE ON TOP

THE SWEETEST SOUNDS

TEN CENTS A DANCE

THERE IS NOTHIN' LIKE
A DAME

THERE'S A SMALL HOTEL

THIS CAN'T BE LOVE

THIS NEARLY WAS MINE

TIME

WAIT TILL YOU SEE HER

WHAT'S THE USE OF WOND'RIN'

WHERE OR WHEN

WITH A SONG IN MY HEART

YOU COULD NOT PLEASE
ME MORE

YOU TOOK ADVANTAGE OF ME

YOU'LL NEVER WALK ALONE

YOU'RE NEARER

YOU'VE GOT TO BE
CAREFULLY TAUGHT

YOUNGER THAN SPRINGTIME

Williamson Music is a registered trademark of the
Trusts and Estates of Richard Rodgers and Oscar Hammerstein II

A Joint Publication of

WILLIAMSON MUSIC®
A RODGERS AND HAMMERSTEIN COMPANY

and

HAL•LEONARD™

U.S. $19.95

ISBN 0-7935-0033-8

0 73999 90422 2

HL00490422

48 34UW2 4922
BR
1/98 72136-83 NULE